My First Hungarian
Fruits & Vegetables

Picture Book with English Translations

Published By: My First Picture Book™

Ever Wondered How That Word Sounds?

We've introduced complimentary audio recordings for all our books to enhance your reading experience. Dive into the sounds at **MyFirstPictureBook.com** and not only read, but also listen and learn.

A Heartfelt Message from Our Publishers:

Your support does more than just buy a book. It uplifts native authors and fuels the dreams of a close-knit business. We value every reader, and your insights could shape our next bestseller! Got suggestions or feedback? Let's co-create magic. Connect with us through the 'Contact Us' section on our website at **MyFirstPictureBook.com**.

Fruits

Apple

alma

ahl-mah

Banana

banán

bah-nahn

Cherry

cseresznye

cher-es-nyeh

Coconut

kókuszdió

koh-koos-dee-oh

Grape

szőlő

ser-loh

Lemon

citrom

tsee-trom

Mango

mangó

mahn-goh

Orange

narancs

nah-rahnch

Papaya

papaja

pah-pah-yah

Peach

őszibarack

ooh-see-ba-rakh

Pear

körte

kur-teh

Pineapple

ananász

ah-nah-nahs

Plum

szilva

seel-vah

Pomegranate

gránátalma

grah-naht-ahl-mah

Raspberry

málna

mahl-nah

Strawberry

eper

eh-per

Watermelon

görögdinnye

gu-rog-deen-nyeh

Vegetables

Aubergine (Eggplant)

padlizsán

pod-lee-zshan

Broccoli

brokkoli

brok-ko-lee

Cabbage

káposzta

kah-pos-tah

Capsicum (Bell Pepper)

paprika

pap-ree-kah

Carrot

sárgarépa

shahr-gah-ray-pah

Cauliflower

karfiol

kar-fee-ol

Celery

zeller

zel-ler

Corn

kukorica

koo-ko-ree-tsa

Cucumber

uborka

oo-bor-kah

Garlic

fokhagyma

fok-hah-dy-mah

Ginger

gyömbér

yum-bair

Mushroom

gomba

gom-bah

Onion

hagyma

hah-dy-mah

Pea

borsó

bor-shoh

Potato

burgonya

boor-gon-yah

Pumpkin

tök

took

Spinach

spenót

shpeh-noht

Tomato

paradicsom

pah-rah-dee-chom

Made in the USA
Monee, IL
05 November 2026

67375723R00024